Back-to-School IDEA BOOK

GRADES 4–6

TREND enterprises, Inc.

Dear Teacher,

You are about to embark on an exciting experience that will inspire both you and the children in your group! Whether you are beginning another incredible year in teaching or meeting your own class for the first time, you will certainly have many exciting challenges.

One of the most important challenges is getting to know each child in the group. As you know, getting to know a new group of children or a child who joins your group during the year is more than just putting faces with names on a list. You'll want to know what makes each individual tick, what is special about each one, and what each will need from you to have a successful year. This *Back-to-School Idea Book* will help you get started. The activities will help you build a well-rounded curriculum to use during the first several weeks of school, at any time during the year when you add a new child to the group, or when you feel you want to build a sense of community in your group. You'll learn about each person's likes and dislikes, find out where individuals excel or have difficulty, discover how individuals relate to each other and to you, and much more.

Use the activities in this book to really get to know each child in your group. The activities relate to the subjects you deal with throughout a regular day or week. They are sure to add to your success as a teacher.

HAVE FUN!

Contents

How to use this book

To help you construct your lesson plans, this book includes several organizational strategies:

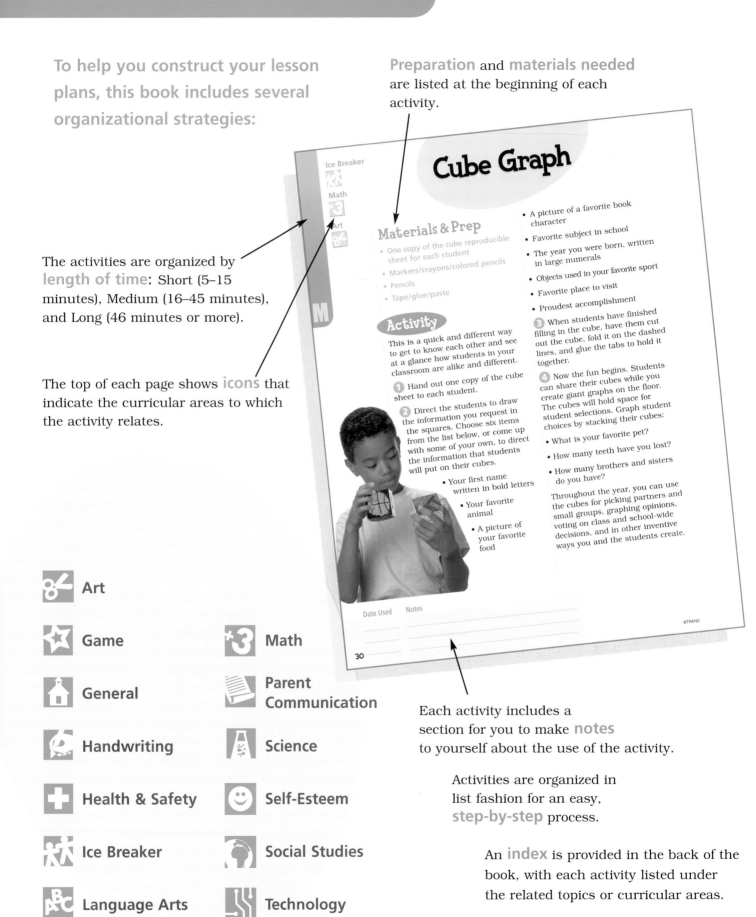

Preparation and materials needed are listed at the beginning of each activity.

Cube Graph

Materials & Prep
- One copy of the cube reproducible sheet for each student
- Markers/crayons/colored pencils
- Pencils
- Tape/glue/paste

Activity

This is a quick and different way to get to know each other and see at a glance how students in your classroom are alike and different.

1. Hand out one copy of the cube sheet to each student.

2. Direct the students to draw the information you request in the squares. Choose six items from the list below, or come up with some of your own, to direct the information that students will put on their cubes.
- Your first name written in bold letters
- Your favorite animal
- A picture of your favorite food
- A picture of a favorite book character
- Favorite subject in school
- The year you were born, written in large numerals
- Objects used in your favorite sport
- Favorite place to visit
- Proudest accomplishment

3. When students have finished filling in the cube, have them cut out the cube, fold it on the dashed lines, and glue the tabs to hold it together.

4. Now the fun begins. Students can share their cubes while you create giant graphs on the floor. The cubes will hold space for student selections. Graph student choices by stacking their cubes:
- What is your favorite pet?
- How many teeth have you lost?
- How many brothers and sisters do you have?

Throughout the year, you can use the cubes for picking partners and small groups, graphing opinions, voting on class and school-wide decisions, and in other inventive ways you and the students create.

Date Used   Notes

30   ©TREND

The activities are organized by length of time: Short (5–15 minutes), Medium (16–45 minutes), and Long (46 minutes or more).

The top of each page shows icons that indicate the curricular areas to which the activity relates.

Each activity includes a section for you to make notes to yourself about the use of the activity.

Activities are organized in list fashion for an easy, step-by-step process.

An index is provided in the back of the book, with each activity listed under the related topics or curricular areas.

- Art
- Game
- General
- Handwriting
- Health & Safety
- Ice Breaker
- Language Arts
- Math
- Parent Communication
- Science
- Self-Esteem
- Social Studies
- Technology

Making Pairs, Groups, and Teams

You are constantly trying to foster a sense of community and teach students the merits of cooperation. One way to do this is to have students work in pairs, groups, or teams. Organizing students into groups can be a very difficult and trying task. Gone are the days of "Captains" picking teams and numbering off "1, 2, 1, 2…" Today's children seem to be more sensitive, and certainly much to smart, for those old strategies. Listed below and on the following pages are some new ways to combine your students. Try the ideas to create random pairs, groups, or teams in fun ways that suit many of your classroom needs.

Playing Cards

Here are a few ways to use playing cards to create groups. You'll probably think of many other ways too. If you have more than 28 kids, adjust as needed.

- To get seven groups of four students each, mix and pass out all four eights, nines, tens, jacks, queens, kings, and aces. Have students find others with the same value cards.

- To get four groups, pass out equal numbers of each suit, such as seven diamonds, seven hearts, seven spades, and seven clubs. Have students find others with the same suit.

- To get pairs, pass out two of each card plus the jokers: two aces, two kings, two queens, two jacks, two jokers, etc. Have students find others with the same card.

Greeting Cards

Greeting cards are an excellent item to save and use in your classroom. To use them to create pairs or groups try these activities.

- Cut greeting cards in 2–,3–,4–,or 5–piece puzzles. Have students put puzzles together to find their groups.

- Get several greeting cards for different holidays, as many holidays as you want groups. Pass them out and have students form groups according to the holiday represented on their cards.

ABCs and 123s

Students' names and ages are very important to them. Try these five ideas for grouping.

- Group students by the first letter in their first or last names.

- Group students by having them find five other people who all have different first letters of their first or last names.

- Use third letters in names, last letters in names, or double letters in names.

- Use birthday dates or months to group students (January = 1, August = 8).

- Assemble all ten-year-olds in one place and all eleven-year-olds in another. Then have them find someone in the other group for a partner.

Make Teams with Teams!

Gather several full team sets of baseball, football, basketball, or other team trading cards. When you have the card sets, try these ways to create groups.

1. All the Pitchers

Hand out the necessary number of cards in as many positions as you would like groups. For example, to make groups of five in a class of 30, pass out five each of six different positions: five pitchers, five catchers, five first basemen, five second basemen, five shortstops, and five third basemen. Then have the students find the people holding the cards with a player who plays the same position as the player on their cards.

2. Make a Team

Pass out the necessary cards for students to create teams of players. Students can match uniforms to find their other team members.

3. Cover Your Bases

Pass out cards from different teams for several positions, as many positions as you want students in a group. Have students find others with cards to complete a full team of players. For example, tell students they must find a pitcher; catcher; first, second, and third basemen; shortstop; and three outfielders. This creates equal groups of nine. If you would like smaller teams, try only using infield players. You could also use trading cards from another sport, such as basketball, which only has five team members on the court at a time.

Choose Your Favorite

Have students choose the things they like and form groups at the same time. This way they'll be in groups and already have something in common with everyone there! To get started, designate different parts of the room for the different options and have students go to the appropriate area. Or, you could graph the options and then have the class split up afterwards. Remember to provide as many options as you would like to have groups. Possible questions may include the following options:

- What is your favorite fast food restaurant?

- What type of pet do you have? (One option is none.)

- What is your favorite sport?

- Which cartoon character do you like the best?

- What is your favorite soft drink?

- Where would you like to vacation?

- Which television show do you like the best?

Families

Pair students by using their families as a vehicle. This important topic can be used as a fun pairing activity.

1. Siblings, Siblings

Have students move to one part of the room if they have a sister, another place if they have a brother, and another place if they don't have any siblings. If they have one of each, use those students to balance the groups, or make them a separate group.

2. Oldest, Middle, Youngest, Only

Separate students using relative position in the family as a grouping technique. Once they are in these groups you can keep them as is or pull one from each group to form the final groups. This can help to even out your groups with leaders, followers, etc.

My favorite fast food restaurant is...

Curriculum Connection

Use the curriculum as a vehicle to form pairs, groups, and teams. The following techniques will reinforce the curriculum and provide fun ways for students to find their place for the next exciting activity.

1. Math

Are you working on multiplication or division facts? Do you want to introduce your students to some basic algebraic principles? These concepts are perfect ways to connect students. Write problems on one set of index cards and answers on another set. Pass the cards out and ask students to make correct problem-answer matches. If you want groups of five, write five different problems that all equal the same answer. Have students find others with identical answers.

2. Language Arts

Use language arts skills to find pairs and teams. Have students pair up by matching index cards—one set with book titles and another set with the authors or illustrators. Prepare synonym cards and make groups by having students find others who have synonyms of the word on their cards. You can gather groups by giving each child one letter on a card and have him or her find the other students with whom they can create a word.

3. Social Studies

The social studies curriculum provides endless possibilities for pairing and grouping. Give half of your students a state and the other half a capital and have them make matches. You can also match countries and capitals. You may also give students names of people in history and have them find other people who worked for the same cause, such as Martin Luther King, Jr., Rosa Parks, and Malcolm X.

Clothing

Are your students wearing buttons, zippers, snaps...? Use their clothing as a means for dividing them into groups.

1. Layers and Sleeves

Are half of your students wearing short sleeves and the other half wearing long? How about layers? Are some wearing only a T-shirt while others sport a T-shirt and a sweatshirt, or button-down shirt and a sweater? Layers and sleeves provide great possibilities for making groups.

2. Fasteners

What types of fasteners are on your students' shirts? How about students' shoes? It's easy to divide kids in many ways using this as a grouping technique. Have the kids with buttons go to one area, those with zippers to another, and students with no fasteners in another area. It's fun to have them compare and find their correct spots.

Multiple Intelligence Learning Centers

Learning centers, based on Howard Gardner's theory of Multiple Intelligences, emphasize students' abilities, rather than inabilities. Children are challenged in areas where they are comfortable, and gently guided to work on intelligences they need to develop. Introduce one center a day and allow students to spend time exploring the activities and learning about the intelligence. Specific tasks geared to your curriculum can be added to the centers at any time. Each of the centers requires different materials. The materials you need will depend on the activities you choose to include.

Word Smart

The Verbal-Linguistic Intelligence Center

Children with strong word smarts love reading, writing, telling stories, and playing word games. When putting together your Word Smart Center, include activities that allow students to explore language, writing, and reading. Here are some ideas of what to include at the Word Smart Center:

- Writing materials, such as pencils; colored pencils; pens; markers; and many types of paper for creating books, including stationery, envelopes, notebook paper, and construction paper.

- A variety of reading materials: library books, magazines, newspapers, crossword puzzles, dictionaries, books related to themes, poems, books with tapes, CD stories, and reference material on computer software. Encourage students to write books and have them "published" for the classroom collection.

- A computer with word processing, bookmarked Internet sites, and software programs that reinforce vocabulary with word games and word searches.

- Word charts and word webs used for building vocabulary and specific themes.

- Many kinds of pointers to make the study of words more fun, such as wands, flyswatters, frames, and flashlights.

- Feature an Author of the Month.

- Commercially made word games, such as Boggle, Scrabble, Taboo, or other popular board games.

Body Smart

The Bodily-Kinesthetic Intelligence Center

Children strong in body smarts think and learn through physical movement and by touching and feeling. They are active and athletic, and may enjoy a variety of activities, including dancing, creative dramatics, running, jumping, building, sculpting, weaving, touching, and gesturing. Here are some ideas of what to include at the Body Smart Center:

- Opportunities for playing charades, story telling with puppets, and making props.
- Ideas on how to adapt books and stories into their own plays.
- Recipes and ingredients to make dough and putty. This provides practice in reading and following directions.
- Construction materials such as wooden blocks and Legos.
- Discarded telephones, radios, and computer components that students can safely take apart and look at. The kids will enjoy using tools like screwdrivers to inspect the "guts" of some items they see every day.
- Space to display student collections, such as a shell collection, when studying about the ocean.
- Computer games that improve manual dexterity.
- Commercial games like Jenga, Twister, and Guesstures.
- Sign language books and posters. Have someone who signs be a guest speaker.

Picture Smart

The Visual and Spatial Intelligence Center

Children strong in picture smarts think in terms of images and pictures. They love designing, inventing, drawing, visualizing, and doodling. Here are some ideas of what to include at the Picture Smart Center:

- Materials such as paint, paint brushes of all sizes, markers, chalk, crayons, colored pencils, scissors, tape, glue, paper of many sizes and colors, stamps and stamp pads, wallpaper samples, yarn, string, and newspaper.
- An easel for painting or drawing large pictures.
- An artist's painting, to encourage students to copy a particular technique.
- Illustrated children's books to study the illustrations and try the different techniques used by the artists.
- A tubful of recycled materials.
- Clay for sculpting.
- A mapping activity, such as drawing a map of ones home, block, or school.
- Jigsaw puzzles, or directions for making one from scratch.
- "How to draw" books to help reinforce following directions.
- Games, including Connect Four, Tic–Tac–Toe, and memory. Pictionary, another commercial game, can easily be adapted to words that go along with themes or skills students are working on.
- Origami paper and instructions.
- Directions for students to illustrate books and covers for stories they have written.

Number Smart

The Logical-Mathematical Intelligence Center

Students with strong number smarts think by reasoning; and they love experimenting, questioning, figuring out logical puzzles, and calculating. Often they are strongest in science and math. Here are some ideas of what to include at the Number Smart Center:

- A microscope, thermometers, magnifying glasses, pattern blocks, calculators, a balance, dominoes, counters, geoboards, graph paper, measuring instruments, tangrams, timer, dice, and spinners.
- Science books that contain experiments, such as *Kid Kapers* by Judith Blumer, *Scienceworks* by Ontario Science Centre, *Thinking Games* by Valerie Anderson, and *Mudpies to Magnets* by Robert Williams.
- Space for children to work together picking out experiments that look interesting to them, collecting materials needed, preparing for a pre-experiment conference with the teacher or adult volunteer, and then doing the experiment.
- An estimation jar. Children take turns bringing in items to fill the jar and then having others estimate how many pieces are in the jar.
- Brain-teaser books.
- Commercial games like Prof. Wacky's Neon Number Flash™, Clue, Monopoly, Checkers, Chess, or card games.
- Computer programs that relate to the logical/mathematical intelligence.

Music Smart

The Musical Intelligence Center

Students strong in music smarts think via rhythm, tone, timbre, and melodies. They love singing, whistling, humming, listening to music, playing instruments, and tapping their hands and feet. Music is used to commit things to memory, and help learn and reinforce concepts. Here are some ideas of what to include at the Music Smart Center:

- Cassette tapes or CDs with a variety of music genres.
- Cassette tapes or CDs of nature sounds, the rain forest, and ocean.
- Opportunities to make up new words for familiar tunes.
- An area where children can record their voices.
- A collection of rhythm instruments.
- Sound identification activities, such as identifying the instruments in music selections.
- Materials to make instruments by following the directions in books. The instruments can later be used as background music for a student play.
- Opportunities for students to play instruments for the class.
- The commercial game Simon that plays a set of notes coded by color.
- Keyboards to practice reading music or composing music.

Nature Smart

The Naturalist Intelligence Center

Students strong in nature smarts are in tune with nature. They may be able to identify different species of plants and animals and may know a lot about our natural environment. Being outdoors, hiking, camping, going on walks or bike rides, are some of the ways nature smart people enjoy spending their time. Here are some ideas of what to include at the Nature Smart Center:

- A microscope and slides of different organisms or plant life.
- Space to display items that students find, or collections they have of rocks, shells, leaves, etc.
- Field guides and other nature books.
- Cassette tapes or CDs of nature sounds.
- Drawing paper, markers, crayons, or colored pencils for drawing landscapes and still-life nature scenes.
- Tempera paints for printing pictures with items collected outside.

Self Smart

Intrapersonal Intelligence Center

Students strong in intrapersonal intelligence know about themselves and are in tune with their minds and bodies. These self smart people enjoy spending time alone with their thoughts, keeping a journal, and other solitary activities. Besides the activities on the previous pages, here are some other activities that may occupy these students:

- A computer for searching the World Wide Web looking for information and topics of interest.
- Paper, cardboard, fabric, and other scrap materials for creating a homemade journal.
- A tape recorder for making recordings of original stories.
- Games such as solitaire, working on puzzles, or other individual games.
- Time to day dream.

People Smart

Interpersonal Intelligence Center

Students strong in interpersonal intelligence are excellent in groups. These people love to be around other people and are the life of the party. People smart individuals enjoy partner and group assignments, being in clubs, and simply spending time with different people. Besides the activities on the previous pages, here are some other activities that may occupy these students:

- Plays to perform for others.
- Opportunities to volunteer with the elderly or help other children.
- Time to plan and attend events or parties.
- Time to share experiences in front of the group and engaging in other speaking opportunities.
- Group games and puzzles.

Who's Who Baby?

Materials & Prep

- One copy of the parent note for each student
- Bulletin board and various board decorations

Prepare a bulletin board with paper and trimmers to display the baby pictures when they arrive.

Activity

Even though your students may still be their parents "babies," they have certainly changed since infancy. This activity is always fun for students and provides many laughs.

1 Prepare a note like this sample to send home to your students' parents at the beginning of the school year.

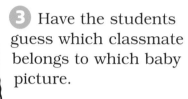

2 When you have collected the photographs, carefully put the child's name on the back of his or her picture with a post-it note. Using an adhesive that will not damage the photos, gently attach them to a bulletin board, door, or poster board for all students to see and discuss.

3 Have the students guess which classmate belongs to which baby picture.

This will bring lots of laughs, stories, and smiles to your class.

Be sure to include your own baby picture and watch the students' faces as you share stories about when you were younger!

FACT: The Pennsylvania Health Department found two very unusual first names in the birth certificates issued in 1979: Pepsi and Cola.

Dear parents and guardians,

Please send with your child a baby picture of him or her for a class project. We will take good care of this prized possession and return it in two weeks. Thank you for your cooperation.

Sincerely,

Mrs. Owen

Date Used   Notes

Apples and Oranges

Materials & Prep

• None

Activity

Things, like people, can be different and alike in many ways. It is beneficial to have students think of things in new and different ways. Try this activity when you have a few minutes to fill.

For the items listed below, have your students name three ways the two items are alike and three ways they are different. Use this example to get started.

A straw hat and a glass of lemonade

Alike:

• They are both used in the summertime.

• They are both yellow.

• My mom likes them both.

Different:

• One you wear, one you drink.

• One is solid, one is liquid.

• I like hats, but I don't like lemonade.

Try to compare these items!

1. a pencil and a stapler

2. a porcupine and a blowfish

3. a cheeseburger and a football

2. licorice and a witch's hat

3. a tree and an ocean

4. a flag and a television

5. an ice cream sundae and a candle

6. a giraffe and a teacher

9. a bike and in-line skates

10. a comic book and a deck of cards

When you use all the ideas printed above, come up with some on your own or have the students choose two items. This practice in creativity can be used as a writing assignment, too. It will be a wonderful addition to any student's writing repertoire.

FACT: Some of the world's deadliest snakes live at the bottom of the ocean.

Date Used   Notes

Who's Left?

Materials & Prep

• None

Activity

This clever game will hone students' abilities to determine attributes.

1 Ask eight students to stand in the front of the room.

2 Tell the rest of the class that you are thinking of one specific student from the group of eight, and they need to try to guess who that might be. You can secretly write down that student's name so you can verify later who it was that you chose.

3 Begin slowly eliminating the students in the front of the class by asking those with specific attributes to return to their seats. Continue doing this until the last student is left. For example, a round might go like this:

• Anyone with red hair can sit down.

• If your shoe is untied, please return to your seat.

• If you ate potato chips at lunch, please be seated.

• If you have an older sister you may sit down.

• If you are on a soccer team, please sit down.

4 After you do this once, you can ask a different group of students to the front of the room. This time, make the same types of statements, but ask the students at the front of the room to remain standing the whole time. Ask the rest of the class to listen and try to determine who you are describing. Can they guess correctly?

5 Once students have had a chance to play a few times, allow one to take the lead and give the clues.

Students will love trying to outwit you and others in this attribute activity!

Date Used   Notes

Write On!

Materials & Prep

- Large coffee can with plastic lid
- Small strips of paper (8½" x 2")
- Pencils
- Chalkboard or white board

Cover the coffee can with colorful paper and label it "Write On!"

Activity

Every student should read, write, and be read to each day. Finding books for you and your students to enjoy is fairly simple, and usually enjoyable. Coming up with writing ideas isn't always so easy. Why not have your students be the ones to come up with those last minute writing ideas, story starters, or journal entries?

Introduce your students to the idea of a "suggestion box" of writing topics. Show them the coffee can you have decorated and labeled "Write On!" At any time they can write an idea on a slip of paper for a story or other writing assignment and drop it in the can. During the year, when individuals or the class need an idea for creative writing, they can pull an idea from the can and use it as the topic of a story.

Start your "idea can" with a bit of class brainstorming to get the creative juices flowing. Ask for writing topics from the kids and list them on the board. You will probably need to contribute some ideas such as these:

A day in the life of a potato.

When I learn to fly I will...

If I were the teacher, I'd...

Juan knew it was his lucky day the moment...

Billy Jo leaned over to pick the flower, but instead found a...

My best friend is great because...

Now ask the students to contribute their ideas to the coffee can by writing ideas on slips of paper. At least once a week, draw an idea from the can for a writing activity. You'll have plenty of ideas to choose from in your can. The next time you put journaling up on the schedule, students will be buzzing about which of their ideas will be selected.

Date Used   Notes

Guess the Classmate

Materials & Prep

- 3" x 5" index cards
- Pencils

Activity

Here is a way to help you get to know your students as they get to know each other.

Give each student three 3" x 5" index cards. Have each student write one interesting fact about himself or herself on each card. Encourage the students to write something that the other students wouldn't necessarily already know about them. Collect the cards and mix them up.

The game can be played a number of different ways.

I'm an excellent tree climber.

1 When you need a five-minute activity before the buses come or music class begins, try this activity. Read off one of the cards from the pile and have the students guess to which classmate that fact belongs. The first one to raise his or her hand and give a correct response wins.
(Wins what? That's up to you.)

2 Another way to use the cards later in the year is in a one-on-one game. Two students stand next to each other. You choose a card and read it. The first of the two students to correctly identify which student wrote that card advances by choosing another student for the next card. See if one student can make it all the way around the entire class.

3 One more way to play is to divide the class into two or more teams. Have one representative from each team go to the board. When a card is read, the first person to correctly write the student's name and put down the chalk wins a point for his or her team.

For added fun, put in some clues about yourself. The students will be thrilled to learn something new about their teacher.

Date Used   Notes

Parent Survey

Materials & Prep

- One copy of the parent questionnaire for each student
- Envelopes

Activity

An excellent way to find out about your students is to ask the folks who know them the best, their parents. It is always best to have some sort of communication with parents and guardians before the first parent-teacher conferences.

Address envelopes to your students' parents and send a questionnaire home with your students for their parents to fill out and return to you. Use the questions in the next column as the basis for your questionnaire. Add specific questions that relate to your school or classroom. Parents are usually willing to tell you about their sons or daughters, and will appreciate the fact that you are interested enough to ask for the information.

Dear Parent,

In order to get to know your child, I would like to gather some information from you. Please take some time to fill out this survey and return it to me in a sealed envelope. Share any information that you believe will help your child and me get to know each other and have a great year!

1. What are your child's general feelings about school?

2. How often do you discuss with your child what he or she is learning in school?

3. What social skills would you like to see your child focus on this year?

4. What educational skills would you like to see your child focus on this year?

5. In what ways can I make this the best possible school year for your child?

6. Do you have any other questions, comments, or concerns?

Please feel free to contact me any time you have a concern or need. I will do my best to make sure that we have the very best school year.

Thank you, *Shari Furlong,*
Your child's teacher

Date Used   Notes

I'm Different!

Materials & Prep

- *The Sneeches* by Dr. Suess (video or book)

You will need to dress up for this activity so that your students can see you in some silly clothes. Wear mismatched clothing, a silly hat, different glasses, and any other items that will make you look different than normal.

Activity

Everyone thinks there's something they do that makes them stand out. The problem is that kids just want to fit in. This activity will give you a chance to act silly in front of your students and in the process, teach them a very valuable lesson.

1 Ask another teacher or assistant at school to greet your students in the morning and help them settle in. Have them begin the normal routine before you arrive.

2 Wait until class has started, and then enter the room acting goofy and apologizing for being so late.

3 Tell the students that you would like them to watch a video, or listen to *The Sneeches*.

4 When the story is over, ask students for feedback using the following questions: Name all of the things that were different about the two different groups of Sneeches. How did the two groups treat each other? Why do you think the Star Bellied Sneeches treated the Sneeches without stars the way they did? Do you think it was fair the way the Sneeches without stars were treated? How did the Star Bellied Sneeches feel when the Sneeches without stars could have stars put on their bellies? What did they do? What happened in the end when they couldn't tell one group from the other? Do you think people ever act like the Sneeches?

5 Next, pair up your students. Have each pair come up with at least five things about themselves that are different from each other.

6 Talk about how even though students are different—some wear glasses, some are of a different race, and some have curly hair—every one is just as important as everyone else and, everyone in the class is a potential friend.

Throughout the year let the Sneeches be an example of working to get along.

Date Used   Notes

All about You

Materials & Prep

• Reproducible (optional)

• Pencils (optional)

Activity

Here is a fun, abstract activity that will enable you to learn more about your students as they discover a little more about themselves. You may use this activity (see reproducible on next page) in one of two ways.

1 Pass out the sheets to students and have each work alone at his or her desk.

2 Ask your students to respond orally to one or two of the groupings each day when you find you have a little time to spare.

3 No matter which version of this activity you use, get your students together to discuss their answers. Ask volunteers to share some reasons for their answers. Have students come up with some other lists of things to compare and see what their answers are and why. Students would probably have fun applying some of these to each other too. (i.e. I think Jodi is like a radio because she likes to play the piano and is a good musician.) You and your students will learn a lot about each other and have fun doing it! They will enjoy thinking about their answers and deciding "what" they are. You may find that some of the explanations for their answers are quite profound.

FACT: Elephants and humans are the only animals that can stand on their heads.

Date Used   Notes

I am like...

Circle the item in each line that is the most like you.

1. construction paper | typing paper | origami paper

2. January | June | September

3. a blue circle | a yellow triangle | a purple diamond

4. whole wheat | soft white | pumpernickel

5. a dandelion | a rose | a water lily

6. a duck | an eagle | a robin

7. peppermint | butterscotch | chocolate

8. a race car | a dump truck | a limousine

9. a book | a newspaper | a magazine

10. a tent | a hotel | an igloo

11. a farm | a jungle | a desert

12. dirty socks | wool cardigan | baseball cap

13. a roller coaster | a merry-go-round | a water slide

14. a mystery novel | a book of poetry | a romantic comedy

15. Superman | George Jetson | Betty Rubble

16. turquoise blue | magenta pink | fire engine red

17. a banana peel | an orange rind | peach fuzz

18. lemonade | hot tea | strawberry shake

19. Michael Jordan | Thomas Jefferson | Mark Twain

20. a reclining chair | a bunk bed | a coffee table

21. a computer | a radio | a television

22. a flower garden | a vegetable garden | a slab of concrete

24. a felt-tipped pen | a #2 pencil | a red magic marker

25. Sunday night | Wednesday afternoon | Monday morning

Back to the Basics

Materials & Prep

- One copy of the "Food Guide Pyramid" sheet for each student

- Food Guide Pyramid reference material

- Crayons, markers, or colored pencils

- Lined paper

- Snack (optional)

Gather food samples to represent each of the food groups. Prepare small pieces for everyone to taste.

Activity

Introduce this activity by having samples of food from each of the areas of the Food Guide Pyramid (fruits; vegetables; meats and other proteins; dairy products; breads and grains; fats, oils, and sweets) for all students to taste. After sufficient tasting, follow these steps for a tasty activity that will help students understand how to eat well, while eating foods that they like.

1 Review or introduce the Food Guide Pyramid with your students. Brainstorm a list of all their favorite foods they enjoy at home, school, Grandma's, or at a restaurant.

2 Figure out where these foods fit into the pyramid categories.

3 Now have the students create their own Food Guide Pyramids on the reproducible sheet provided. Students can fill in each section of the pyramid with all of the foods they like to eat. Give students the option to draw pictures of the foods in each group.

4 On the back of the sheet, have students create a days worth of meals they would like to prepare or eat, including the necessary amounts of food from each group.

5 Read some of the meals to the rest of the class and have them raise their hands if they would like that meal too.

6 At the end of the activity, share a fun, easy, and healthy snack you like to eat with the students. This will give them a good idea of a snack they might be able to make for themselves after school.

FACT: The average child will eat 15 lbs. of cereal in one year.

Date Used   Notes

Food Guide Pyramid

Name _____

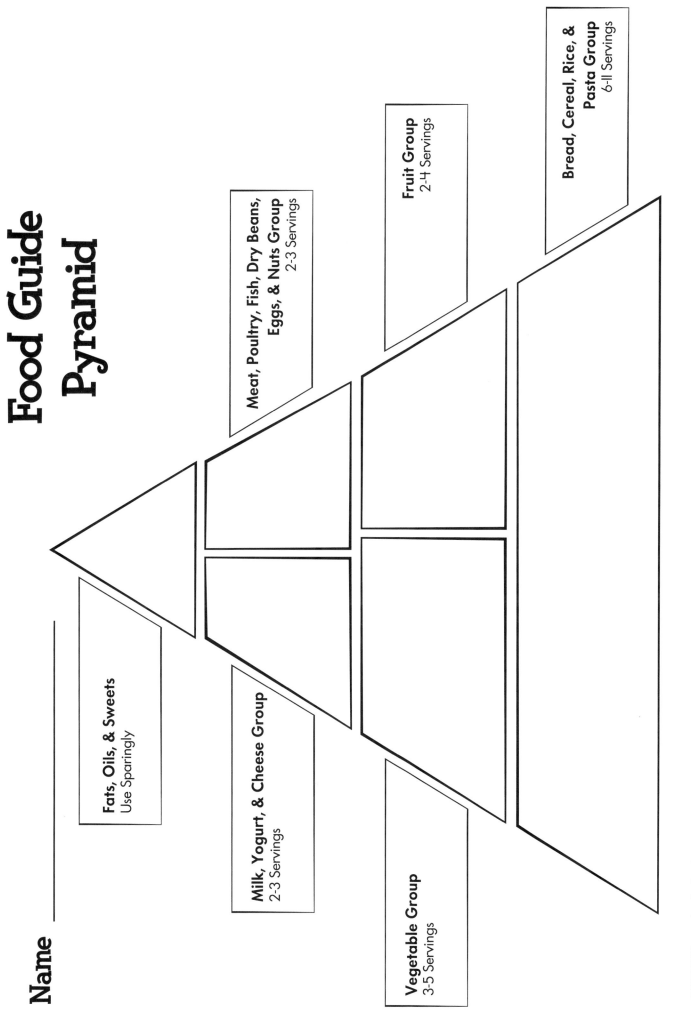

Fats, Oils, & Sweets
Use Sparingly

Milk, Yogurt, & Cheese Group
2-3 Servings

Meat, Poultry, Fish, Dry Beans, Eggs, & Nuts Group
2-3 Servings

Vegetable Group
3-5 Servings

Fruit Group
2-4 Servings

Bread, Cereal, Rice, & Pasta Group
6-11 Servings

Use Your Senses

Materials & Prep

- Storybooks
- Pencils (optional)
- Lined paper (optional)

Gather several storybooks from your classroom or library.

Activity

A good author will often use all five senses to completely give the reader a feeling of what a character is experiencing in a story.

1 Identify with your students the five senses. Have them come up with a descriptive sentence about your classroom for each of the five senses. Here's one example:

The sun beamed through the open window, causing me to shut my eyes. (sight)

The garbage can was full and gave off a musty odor. (smell)

The 2:30 bell rang loudly to end another school day. (sound)

Mr. Gray tapped my shoulder to let me know I got the right answer. (touch)

Our milk at lunch was sweet and fresh. (taste)

2 As an added challenge, try to connect the descriptive sentences into one short story.

3 You may also ask the students to search through a book they are currently reading, or one you assign, and locate ways in which the author uses the five senses to illustrate the story. Have the students find and write, or share orally, three quotes from the book and the corresponding page number for each of the five senses.

Experiences such as this one are wonderful ways to get your students on the road to being better writers. It's fun to watch them improve and learn how to be better storytellers.

FACT: Rats rely predominantly on smell, taste, touch, and hearing as opposed to vision. They move around mainly in the dark, using their long sensitive whiskers and the guard hairs on their body to guide them.

Date Used   Notes

Get Off My Back

Materials & Prep

- 3" x 5" index cards
- Black marker
- Tape or safety pins

Prepare the cards by printing the name of a famous person on each card. Use names that your students would likely recognize. (Some examples are George Washington, Pochahontas, Laura Ingalls Wilder, Dr. Seuss, Christopher Columbus, Sally Ride, Dr. Martin Luther King Jr., Alexander Graham Bell, or Bill Cosby.)

Activity

Here is a fun problem-solving activity for your students that involves thoughtful communication.

1 Tape or pin one of the prepared index cards on the back of each student. Do this without the student knowing whose name is printed on the card. To start the game, no one is to know what name is on his or her back.

2 Students must go around the room asking only yes or no questions of their classmates to figure out the famous person. This activity is great any time of the year to help students communicate with each other. It gets them to start thinking of different ways of describing people, animals, or objects.

Am I a famous rock-n-roll musican?

Mark Twain

FACT: Everyone knows that Donald Duck's nephews are Huey, Dewey, and Louie, but does anyone remember that Mickey Mouse has nephews too? Their names are Mortie and Ferdie.

Date Used   Notes

Planning Ahead

Materials & Prep

- Lined paper
- Pencils
- Markers/crayons
- Envelopes

Activity

"Welcome" is one thing every student likes and needs to hear when returning to school or entering a new classroom. Besides the usual ways to do this each year, try this idea at the end of the school year.

In the spring, have your class reflect on their year in your class. What did they like about it? What was their favorite memory? Who were their best friends? Once you have them in this reflective mode, have them write letters to the new students entering that grade next year. The letters will be on the desks the following fall to welcome the new class members to the room. Each letter will be individualized, created especially for the new occupant of that desk. The letter should include some of the following ideas and whatever else you choose to add.

- A big, friendly "Welcome!"
- An explanation of the class schedule.
- Information about their new teacher.
- Field trips and activities they can look forward to.
- A few thoughts about rules to follow.
- Information on class traditions.
- Anything else interesting or important.

You might want to ask a few students to write two letters just in case you have more students next year than this year. That way everyone can get a personal letter from a past student. If you have extras, use them for new students that enter your class throughout the year.

Keep the letters safely tucked away until the first day of the new school year. Then you can place one "Welcome" letter on top of each desk in your room.

Welcome!

Date Used   Notes

Learning Buddies

Materials & Prep

• **Materials will vary**

Find another teacher with students younger than your students who would like to pair with your class for the year.

Activity

Teaming an older class with a younger class has many benefits. Problems on the playground and during bus rides can be reduced. Students get to know each other and watch out for each other. Older students gain confidence while younger students get more one-on-one attention from "cool," older kids.

1 Find a teacher to work with who teaches a grade that would complement your students' level. Get together to match students. Take into account work habits, need, and ability levels. Be aware that there may be some younger students who are stronger readers than those in your grade. Be careful to make choices that benefit both students.

2 The first time the students are paired, have them interview each other with questions they've written to get to know each other. From there, plan a weekly or monthly meeting time, whatever your schedules can afford.

3 The second time the classes meet, plan activities that allow for interaction, such as floor puzzles and memory or matching games. Watch how certain personalities work with each other. This will give you good insight into the maturity of your students. It will also allow you to see if changes need to be made with the groupings to make the experience optimal for everyone.

Here are some ideas for future sessions together:

• Older students make games to reinforce basic skills at partners' grade level, and then play the games together.

• Take pictures of partners and make frames to display them.

• Read stories to each other.

• Write and illustrate stories together.

Students in both groups will form bonds, and they will have a chance to see various situations and events from another person's point of view.

Date Used   Notes

Skip the Boring Words

Materials & Prep

- One copy of "Skip the Boring Words" reproducible for each student

- One thesaurus for each student or every two students (optional)

- Pencils

Activity

Are you tired of reading the words "good" and "nice" in your students' writing assignments? Let them know right off the bat this year that there are other, more interesting descriptive words in the English language. You will expect them to explore and use descriptive words in assignments that take their writing beyond boring. There are several ways to help your students discover how to "spice" up their writing.

1 The best way to learn how to write descriptively is to read good literature where the author goes into great detail to describe places, people, and things. Choose selections, from books that you enjoy, to read out loud. Allow students to bring in selections from books that they have that also do a good job of descriptive writing.

2 A quick, eye-opening word worksheet is "Skip the Boring Words." This will help your students think about using exciting words. Use the word "happy" and complete an example with your students on the board. Then let them go off on their own, or with partners, to complete the worksheet. Have students come up with six synonyms for "happy." Then have the students write a boring sentence, followed by a new and improved sentence or two.

Students will enjoy finding interesting ways to "Skip the Boring Words."

3 After your students have some experience in writing using interesting synonyms, have them do a short writing activity where they describe something with which they are very familiar. They may choose to describe their house, a tree, a sneaker, their favorite meal, etc. Encourage them to make this so descriptive that the reader will be able to touch, taste, feel, hear, or smell what they are describing. It should be as if the reader is in the room or holding the object that is being described.

Your students will find that their writing will significantly improve when they begin thinking about how to "Skip the Boring Words."

Date Used   Notes

Skip the Boring Words

Name _____

1. Fill in the spaces next to each word with interesting synonyms. Use a thesaurus if you need help coming up with words.

2. For each "boring" word, create a boring sentence, and then fix it with your NEW & IMPROVED words.

1. Nice: _____ _____ _____

_____ _____ _____

Boring: _____

NEW & IMPROVED _____

_____

_____

2. Good: _____ _____ _____

_____ _____ _____

Boring: _____

NEW & IMPROVED _____

_____

3. Small: _____ _____ _____

_____ _____ _____

Boring: _____

NEW & IMPROVED _____

_____

4. Fun: _____ _____ _____

_____ _____ _____

Boring: _____

NEW & IMPROVED _____

_____

Cube Graph

Materials & Prep

- One copy of the cube reproducible sheet for each student
- Markers/crayons/colored pencils
- Pencils
- Tape/glue/paste

Activity

This is a quick and different way to get to know each other and see at a glance how students in your classroom are alike and different.

1 Hand out one copy of the cube sheet to each student.

2 Direct the students to draw the information you request in the squares. Choose six items from the list below, or come up with some of your own, to direct the information that students will put on their cubes.

- Your first name written in bold letters
- Your favorite animal
- A picture of your favorite food
- A picture of a favorite book character
- Favorite subject in school
- The year you were born, written in large numerals
- Objects used in your favorite sport
- Favorite place to visit
- Proudest accomplishment

3 When students have finished filling in the cube, have them cut out the cube, fold it on the dashed lines, and glue the tabs to hold it together.

4 Now the fun begins. Students can share their cubes while you create giant graphs on the floor. The cubes will hold space for student selections. Graph student choices by stacking their cubes:

- What is your favorite pet?
- How many teeth have you lost?
- How many brothers and sisters do you have?

Throughout the year, you can use the cubes for picking partners and small groups, graphing opinions, voting on class and school-wide decisions, and in other inventive ways you and the students create.

Date Used   Notes

©TREND

I. Cut on solid lines.

2. Fold on dashed lines.

3. Glue tabs to form box.

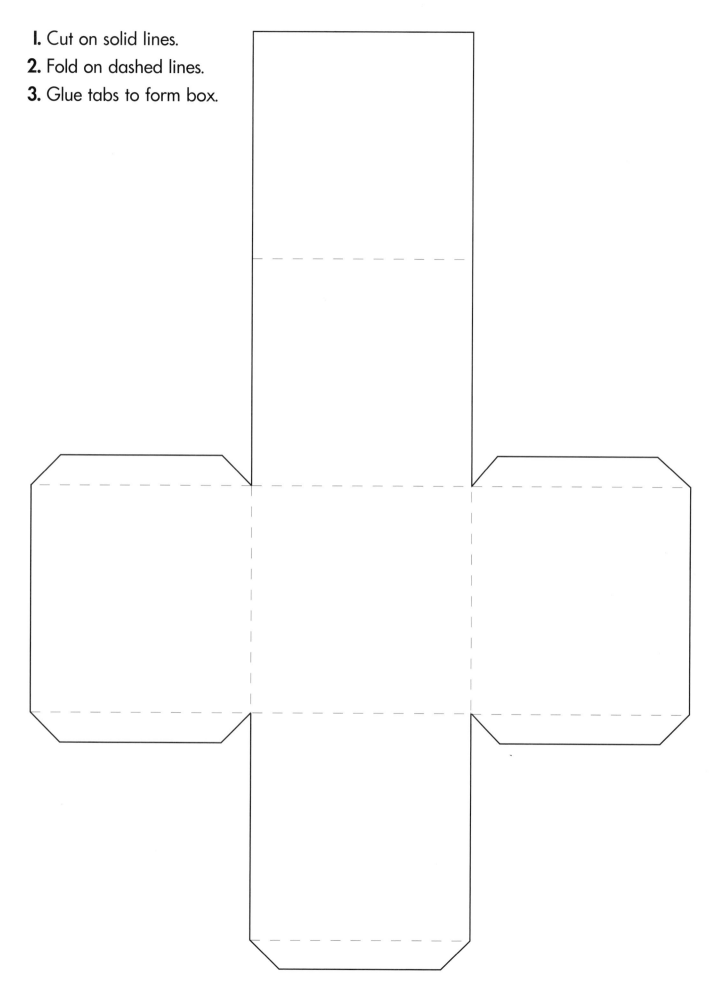

Apple Puzzles

Materials & Prep

• Two washed apples per student

• Apple corer

• Ten child-safe knives, (such as pumpkin-carving knives)

• Lemon juice

• New paint brushes

• Gummy worms (two per student)

Practice your own apple carving before trying it with the class.

Activity

Students will use problem-solving skills to create apple puzzles to share with their friends. Have plenty of extra apples on hand. This is a challenging activity that may require several attempts for some students.

1 Using a corer, core an apple nearly to the bottom. Remove the core and cut off the top half-inch. Discard the remaining core, keeping the top for use later. In order to save class time, you could perform this step prior to the session.

2 Demonstrate how to carve the apple into 4-7 interlocking pieces. Then have the students try to make their own carvings. It may take more than one apple for each student. Save the failed attempts for snacks.

3 When the apples are carved, students then disassemble the pieces and paint the edges and the top piece of the core with lemon juice to prevent browning.

4 Reassemble the puzzles, making sure that the pieces fit together nicely. Before putting the core top on, have each child hide a gummy worm in the core cavity.

5 Now the class must decide to whom to give the puzzles. Consider these options:

• Students may exchange their apple puzzles in class and try to solve them.

• This may be a nice way for your class to introduce themselves to a class of younger students with whom you are pairing for the year. The younger students could take the puzzles apart and find the surprise in the middle. Then they can put it back together again.

• Students can bring the apple puzzles home for parents or siblings to solve.

• These apples make nice gifts for staff members during National Education Week.

Date Used   Notes

To Tell the Truth

Materials & Prep

• A prize for the winner (optional)

Activity

Students won't believe that you are actually allowing them to tell a lie in this laugh-filled activity! Explain to the class that it can be easier to remember names if you learn something interesting about the person who is being introduced. In this activity, students reveal two things about themselves, only one of which is true. The rest of the class will get a chance to guess which statement is true and which is false.

1 Students take turns introducing themselves to the class. Besides stating their names, students are to share one strange-but-true thing about themselves and one thing that is not true about themselves. A student might say, "I was an extra in a movie this summer," and "I have a pet boa constrictor."

2 After each student makes his or her two statements, each of the remaining class members casts a vote for the statement believed to be the truth. The teacher or a student can keep a tally of the votes on the chalkboard. When the votes are counted, the speaker reveals which statement is true. Give the speaker a brief opportunity to explain more about the true statement and field questions.

3 At the conclusion of all the introductions, the child who stumped the most people is declared the winner. The prize? How about a bottle of "truth serum" ...flavored juice with a teacher-made label!

Ms. Jones' TRUTH Serum

Date Used   Notes

Hoop It Up!

Materials & Prep

- Two 12' lengths of rope
- Venn Diagram reproducibles (copy double sided)
- Markers/crayons/colored pencils
- Magazines (optional)
- Glue/paste (optional)

Activity

Students will learn more about Venn Diagrams and about each other in this dynamic activity.

1 Start by laying two rope circles side by side with a few inches of space between them.

2 Choose eight students to stand near the circles. Ask those with brothers to stand in the left circle. Then ask those with sisters to stand in the right circle. It may help to label the circles with index cards.

3 At this point, a student may point out that she or he has brothers and sisters (especially if you purposely choose a participant who has siblings of both genders). Ask your students how to deal with this problem. Can anyone figure out how to include this person in the activity? Of course, to "fix" the problem all you need to do is overlap the circles so the person with both a brother and a sister can stand in the area that overlaps.

4 Now you can make several more life-sized Venn Diagrams by asking different questions that will help you and your students learn more about each other. Try these questions:

- Whose family has a car? Whose family has a truck or van?

- Who likes pizza? Who likes spaghetti?

- Who has a cat? Who has a dog?

5 Students can use the reproducible sheet to create their own Venn Diagrams. You can give them topics, such as things that are red and things that are blue, or things that are plastic and things that are metal. Have students draw pictures, use words, or use magazine pictures to fill in their diagrams. After completing some diagrams where you have chosen the category, they will probably be eager to choose and illustrate some of their own categories.

Date Used   Notes

Venn Diagrams

Name _____

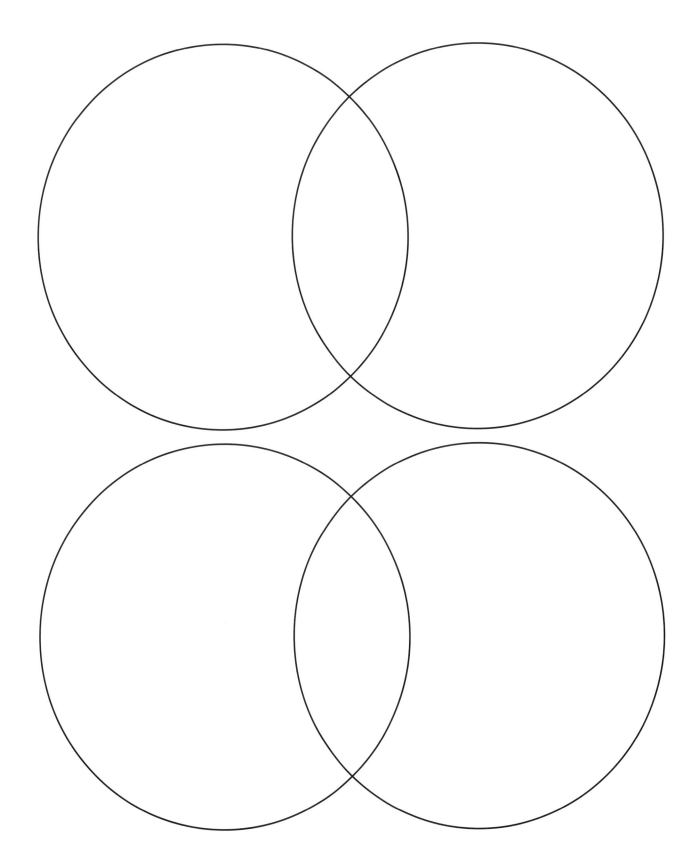

Look into My Crystal Ball!

Materials & Prep

- Lined paper
- Pencils
- Overhead projector (optional)

Activity

Predicting what will happen next is an excellent writing and reading skill. The creativity involved in this process is essential to writing. Use this activity to get those creative juices flowing with your students.

1 Put the story starters below on an overhead transparency or on the board. Add additional ones if you so choose.

2 Have each student choose three different starters from the list to start three different stories or paragraphs. Ask the students to think about their sentences and predict what could happen next. Then have them write a short paragraph or story telling what happened. Encourage creative and humorous answers.

- The phone rang while I was in the bathtub.
- My little brother ate my goldfish.
- We both wore the exact same outfit to the dance.
- I caught the ball just as I was about to be tackled.
- I said I'd be happy to baby sit the twins.
- I woke up at midnight to the sound of running water.
- I packed my suitcase and yelled, "I'm out of here!"
- A big package was delivered with my name on it.
- I looked in the mirror and saw that I had green teeth!
- I found a hundred-dollar bill on the sidewalk.

3 When the students are done with their stories or short paragraphs, ask volunteers to share their writing with the class. Did any of them come up with exactly the same conclusion? How did they arrive at their ideas? Have fun comparing stories and talking about everyone's creative minds.

Date Used   Notes

Michelangelo the Great

Materials & Prep

- 12" x 17" white construction paper
- Crayons/markers/paints/chalk
- Prints of Michelangelo's art

Activity

This activity will not only give your students an appreciation of Michelangelo's work on the dome of the Sistine Chapel, but it will also allow them to see things from a different perspective.

1 Share with your class some prints of Michelangelo's paintings and sculptures. Explain that from 1508 to 1512, Michelangelo painted the ceiling of the Sistine Chapel while lying on his back! Stress to the students that this was long before electrical lights, reclining chairs, or magic markers. Discuss some of the obstacles he must have had to overcome to complete this amazing masterpiece.

2 Give each student a sheet of white construction paper and paints, crayons, chalk, or markers. Before the students go to town creating masterpieces of their own, tape the paper on the underside of their desks or tables. They must lie on their backs to create their works of art.

3 When finished, discuss the students' impressions of working this way. What difficulties did they encounter?

4 You'll find that students will begin to understand what it is like to be challenged in a different way. Remind your students of this activity throughout the year as they try new things and fail. Everyone needs practice.

FACT: Michelangelo was only 24 when he carved the Pieta. It is the only work he ever signed.

Date Used   Notes

My Time Capsule

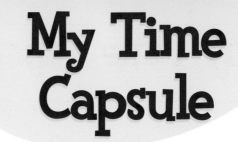

Materials & Prep

- Two copies of the "Time Capsule" reproducible for each student

- Pencils

- Something to hold students' "Time Capsule" sheets: tubes from wrapping paper or paper towels, etc.

- Tape

- Construction paper (optional)

- Markers/crayons (optional)

Activity

This activity provides a fun way for the students to get to know each other. It also gives you a quick reference to students' skill levels as they start the year.

1 Have the children fill in the "Time Capsule" sheet with information about themselves. Use the information to get to know one another in class.

2 Then, seal the sheets inside a container to be opened the last week of school. Potato chip cans, gift wrap tubes, or paper towel tubes taped on the ends make great containers. Students may enjoy decorating the containers by wrapping them and adding fun pictures or art.

3 Before opening the time capsules during the last week of school, have students fill in a second "Time Capsule" sheet to see how much they have changed over the year. At the end of the activity talk to your students about how much things change over a year. Discuss other changes that have gone on in the community or world over the past several months.

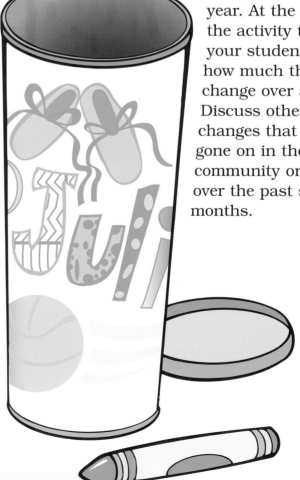

Date Used   Notes

My Time Capsule

This is a record of my life on ___/___/___

Name   Age

My address _____

_____

★ **My best friend** _____

★ **My favorite food** _____

★ **My favorite song** _____

★ **My favorite color** _____

★ **My favorite book** _____

★ **My favorite game** _____

★ **My favorite place to visit** _____

★ **My favorite sport** _____

★ **My best subject** _____

★ **I would like to improve** _____

★ **I would like to learn about** _____

_____

_____

Puzzling Mystery

Materials & Prep

- Drawing or construction paper
- Crayons/markers/colored pencils
- Envelopes
- Scissors

Activity

This activity will be a fun, creative way for your students to get to know each other better.

1 Give each student a sheet of drawing or construction paper. Have students completely fill their sheets with a collage that describes themselves. The paper could include a family portrait, an illustration of a favorite sport, a self-portrait, etc. Make sure that the sheets are totally filled with color and illustration.

2 When the collages are complete, have each student cut his or her paper into 15-20 pieces. Let students know that interesting, curvy lines will be better for the end result than a bunch of triangles or squares.

3 When the puzzles are complete, have each student put her or his puzzle in an envelope and seal it.

4 Collect the envelopes, mix them up, and pass them back to the class. Have students open the envelopes they've been given and put the puzzles together.

Students will enjoy trading these puzzles as many times as you let them. When you're done, keep these around for students to pick up and use throughout the year.

Date Used   Notes

Personalized License Plates

Materials & Prep

- One license plate sheet (6" x 9" light-colored construction paper) for each student
- Scissors or paper cutter
- Markers/crayons/colored pencils

Activity

This is a winning art project that makes a fun name tag for each child's desk.

1 Begin by discussing license plates and how they look. Talk about driving vacations students may have taken and see if they can remember any plates that they saw. What does your states' plate look like? Why does it have the picture on it that it does? What are "vanity" plates? *(Plates that make a word or saying such as, SOCCER, MY TOY, or C YA LTR.)*

2 Give each child a 6" x 9" piece of light-colored construction paper. (Cut 9" x 12" sheets of construction paper in half to have enough 6" x 9" pieces for each student to have one.)

3 Use the sample license plates shown here as examples, or allow the students to come up with a template for the class. Have the children fill in this information: name, school name, teacher's name, school year.

Have students color their plates in a way that makes them unique.

Extension: Give each student another piece of construction paper and allow him or her to make a fun plate to go next to the other one. These vanity plates will help you learn more about your students and encourage creativity.

Date Used   Notes

The Power of Four

Materials & Prep

- One copy of "The Power of Four" reproducible for each student
- Pencils

Activity

This is a fun way to assess the students' command of basic facts along with problem solving skills.

1 Talk about the different operations used to solve math problems. Sometimes you might subtract, add, multiply, or divide. Other times, you may have to use a combination of these operations, which the students do in this activity.

2 Hand out the work sheet that is provided (see reproducible). Have the students use the four 4s to create equations that result in answers from 0 to 20. They can use any of the four operations, use parentheses, combine the numbers (44), or put the fours into fraction form (4/4).

3 Do a couple of equations together on the board to give the students some ideas: 4+(4-4)+4=8, or (4+4)-(4+4)=0. Then let the students work individually or in pairs to finish the page. When finished, share answers with the class.

4 Try this same activity with three 3s or five 5s. What new challenges can your students create?

Extension: Try these other fun math number games to see how numbers and operations work together to create some awesome effects.

1. Hidden Number: Have a friend write down a number between 1 and 99. Next, on the paper, have the friend multiply the number by 2, add 35, multiply by 5, subtract 155, multiply by 10, subtract 200, and tell you what the final answer is. Then simply take off the numbers in the ones and tens columns and what is left is the original number!

2. Palindromes: Adding a number to its reverse will eventually create a palindrome (A number that is the same when read forwards or backwards.) Write down a number. Next, add the reverse of that number to it (e.g. 598 + 895), take the answer and add the reverse of that number, continue to do this until the answer you arrive at is a palindrome.

Date Used   Notes

The Power of 4

4   4   4   4 = _____   4   4   4   4 = _____

4   4   4   4 = _____   4   4   4   4 = _____

4   4   4   4 = _____   4   4   4   4 = _____

4   4   4   4 = _____   4   4   4   4 = _____

4   4   4   4 = _____   4   4   4   4 = _____

4   4   4   4 = _____   4   4   4   4 = _____

Caught in a Brainstorm

Materials & Prep

- Paper strips
- Writing paper (optional)
- Pencils (optional)
- A hat

Before using this activity, prepare the paper strips by writing a category on each (see #1 below)

Activity

Get your students thinking with this fun brainstorming activity. This lesson will engage all students and get them to stretch their thinking and classification skills in a fun and imaginative way.

Things found in the jungle

Types of transportation

Musical instruments

1 Place the paper strips with different categories written on them into a hat.

Categories may include the following:

Things found in the jungle
Things found in the forest
Things found in the desert
Things found in the tundra
Foods that begin with A
Animals that live in the rain forest
Games people play
Types of careers
Things that float

Cities or towns in your state
Animals that live in the ocean
Types of transportation
Musical instruments
Things found on a playground
Things made of wood
Things that roll

Have a student draw a category from the hat. Then students take turns listing different items that apply to the category. Have a volunteer tally answers on the board.

2 As common answers dwindle, encourage students to dig deep to come up with more unusual items to add to the list. Remind students to try not to duplicate answers.

3 As an option, have students write their brainstorm ideas on paper, either working with a partner or on their own. Then compare lists and see how many answers they came up with that others did not.

This activity is an excellent time filler and can be used in any number of ways throughout the school year. Brainstorming is a valuable research tool, and each opportunity to practice will help students as they search for information throughout the year and beyond.

Date Used   Notes

Save Those Receipts

Materials & Prep

- One grocery store receipt per student
- One calculator per student
- Coupons (optional)
- Grocery store advertising flyers (optional)

For several days prior to this activity, ask students to bring in grocery store receipts.

Activity

Ordinary grocery store receipts can inspire a wealth of math and nutrition activities!

1 When you have at least one store receipt for each student, distribute the receipts and ask your students questions that can be answered using the receipts:

- What is the sum of the first ten items on the list?

- What is the sum of the taxable items? You may need to show students how these are noted on the receipt, often with an asterisk.

- How much was spent on fruit? How much was spent on vegetables? How much was spent on produce altogether?

- Circle the items from the grain section of the food pyramid. How much did those items cost in total?

- Underline the junk food prices. How much was spent on these items?

2 If you desire, you can also use assorted coupons and supermarket flyers, including the information in your questions. Let students correct their own work, using calculators.

Use this activity throughout the year to work with your students on consumer skills, and as a fun change of pace.

Date Used   Notes

Tic-Tac-Toe

Materials & Prep

- Physical education vests or papers with X's and O's on them for each class member

- Nine chairs

- Questions you have formulated on a topic you would like to review with your class

Activity

This familiar game can be used as a vehicle for reviewing and assessing many skills.

1 Decide what material you will review or use to challenge your students. It may be one of these topics:
- spelling words
- math facts
- mystery characters from a book or story
- history test review
- trivia questions

2 Divide the class into two equal teams.

3 Teams should be easy to identify. Use team vests from the Physical Education Department or tape papers to each player's back marked with an X for one team and an O for the other team.

4 Arrange nine chairs in the traditional Tic-Tac-Toe pattern, and have each team sit or stand in a straight line near the chairs.

5 Decide which team will go first and then ask the first person in that line a question. If the student gives the correct answer, he or she may choose a chair. If the student answers incorrectly, he or she must go to the end of the line. Now it is the other teams turn.

6 The team that gets three people in a row horizontally, vertically, or diagonally wins the game.

The most exciting aspect of this game is the emphasis on the whole team, not each individual's answer. It is also an excellent way to review because all players will hear the questions and answers, helping them study one more time before the "big test."

Extension: To make the game last longer and add more strategy, add more chairs to create a larger "game board." Players would then have to get four or five in a row to win.

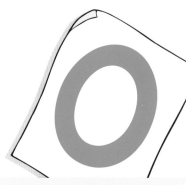

Date Used   Notes

How Do I Measure Up?

Materials & Prep

- Large roll of newsprint or butcher paper (if not in school supplies, check with your local newspaper for a free end roll of newsprint)
- Markers or crayons
- Rulers/measuring tapes with inches and centimeters

Activity

Students will have fun as they practice measuring skills in this artsy activity.

1 Pairs of students take turns lying down on large pieces of newsprint. Partners trace around each other, creating life-sized shapes.

2 Students then measure the body parts—arms, feet, legs, etc.— and write the measurements on the outline. Measure with rulers or tape measures.

Make this activity more challenging by including circumference measurements, such as head and waist, or by requiring students to record measurements using two different units, such as inches and centimeters.

3 Encourage the students to add fun final touches to their outlines, such as hair, clothing, and facial features.

Your students get a chance to practice both measurement and socialization skills, and the finished products look great displayed in the hallway!

Date Used   Notes

Make Your Own Stationery

Materials & Prep

- One computer for each student
- Computer word processing or drawing program
- Computer clip art program (optional)

Activity

Personalized stationery is a wonderful thing for anyone to have for sending notes to a teacher, parents, or friends. This activity will allow the students to learn about the computer, while making their own page of stationery to be printed as needed throughout the year.

1 Have students open the word processing or drawing program you would like them to use. They may need to reduce the page to 50% size to see the whole page.

2 Encourage the students to create a border around the page being careful to allow for enough room to write when they use the stationery.

3 Have students type their names and whatever other information they want at the top of the page. Highlight, enlarge, bold, and center the type.

4 As an option, students can personalize the stationery with items from a clip art program or their own art.

Now each student has his or her own stationery to use throughout the year.

Date Used   Notes

Round Robin Math

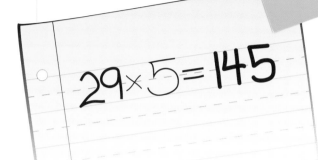

Materials & Prep

- Lined paper
- Pencils

Activity

This is a great way to briefly assess your students' math skills at the beginning of the school year, as well as a fun, quick time-filler any time during the year.

1 Arrange students in groups of five. Tell them that each person will contribute one part of an equation.

2 The first student writes a number, such as 29, and passes the paper to the next child.

3 The second child writes an operational sign, such as x, and passes the paper.

4 The third student writes another number, such as 5, and passes the paper.

5 The fourth student writes an equals sign and passes the paper.

6 The fifth student writes the answer (145).

7 To build cooperation skills with your students, require teams to all agree that the equation is correct before moving on to create another equation. Repeat the activity enough times so that every student has a chance to write each part of the equation.

As you circulate around the room, it will become apparent to you which students need to work on their computational skills.

To turn this into a competitive game, see which team can create the most correct equations in a set period of time. Students will have so much fun, they won't realize this is a learning drill!

Date Used   Notes

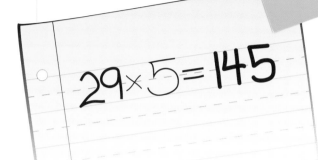

Autograph Bingo

Materials & Prep

- One copy of your Bingo grid for each student

- Index cards with each student's name on a card

- Pencils

- Small pieces of paper for Bingo markers

Determine the number of students in your class and create a grid that will accommodate each student's name. Use your name and the names of other school personnel to round out your grid so that it is a square. Don't forget to make one calling card for each name on the grids.

Activity

Children learn each others' names as they collect autographs of their classmates on a Bingo card. Then they'll reinforce the learning as they play Autograph Bingo.

1 Hand a Bingo grid to each student. Ask them to move about to collect a signature in each square from each member of the class. Each person should sign a square on every grid, including his or her own. Remind students to vary the location in which they write their names. If you used names of staff people, fill in those names ahead of time.

2 When every sheet is filled, ask students to check that they have every student's signature. Now have them sit down for the game.

3 Determine what kind of Bingo students will need to get for each game before it starts: four corners, horizontal, vertical, diagonal, etc.

4 As you call names from the pile of index cards, ask each student to stand when his or her name is called. This will help you and the other children put a name to a face. Students cover the names called with paper or a marker.

5 When a student has covered the correct spaces for Bingo, she or he calls out "BINGO!" Have the student read off the covered names for the Bingo to verify the win. Then play again with everyone.

This game is an excellent one to bring out when you have a few minutes to spare during your day.

Date Used   Notes

Grid Locked

Materials & Prep

- Construction paper
- Pencils
- Markers/crayons

Activity

Here is a fresh name game activity for your students.

1 Across the top of a piece of paper have each student write his or her name, either first or last name depending on skill level and/or length of their name.

2 Leave a 1" margin on the left side of the paper. In between the letters, draw vertical lines to the bottom of the page.

3 In the far left column, have the students write the following list of nouns or create their own list:

- Color
- Animal
- Country
- Famous Person
- Seven-letter word

4 Have the students draw horizontal lines across the page between the nouns. Once the grids are drawn, the students can fill in the squares by naming items that begin with the corresponding letters of their names. Use the example below to get the students started.

	H	A	N	S
Color	Huckleberry	Amber	Nectar	Silver
Animal	Horse	Aardvark	Night owl	Skunk
Country	Honduras	Austria	Netherlands	Sweden
Famous person	Harry Truman	Jane Austin	Neil Armstrong	Shel Silverstein
Seven-letter word	Hurried	Authors	Nickels	Studied

Date Used   Notes

Be a Follower

Materials & Prep

- One copy of the Worksheet reproducible for each student
- Pencils

Activity

This activity gives much-needed practice in following directions.

1 Explain that the class will be doing a silent activity. Students should carefully follow all of the directions on the list, then read quietly until everyone is done.

2 Have each student sit at his or her desk. Then, pass out the Worksheet. Allow students to work for about 15 minutes.

3 Students who do this activity properly will have only their names written on the papers. How many students did you "catch" not following directions?

4 After all of the students have finished, in one way or another, bring them together for a discussion about listening and following directions. Ask them the following questions, along with any of your own:

- Did all of you follow the directions?

- For those of you who didn't, what happened as a result of not following the directions?

- Are directions always important? Have the students talk about different problems that could arise when people don't follow directions.

- What can you do to get better at listening and following directions in the future?

Besides being able to laugh about themselves, students will learn an important lesson about listening and following directions.

FACT: If each count were one second long, it would take about twelve days to count to a million and thirty-two years to count to a billion.

Date Used   Notes

Worksheet

Name_____

1. Read through all of the directions on this page before doing anything else.

2. Circle all of the numbers on this page.

3. Fold this paper in half horizontally, then unfold it.

4. Draw a smile face on the back of this paper.

5. Write your birth date in the lower right corner of this page.

6. Add your age + your shoe size + the day of the month (i. e. 27).
   Then multiply that number by the number of brothers and sisters you have.

7. If you believe you have followed all of the directions to this point,
   stand up and say "I have!"

8. Put a hat on the smile face on the back of this page.

9. Write the alphabet in the left margin of this page.

10. Write one complete sentence about the shirt you are wearing.

11. Write your name in the space at the top of this paper and do not complete any of the other questions. You are finished!

Cartoon Hunt

Materials & Prep

- Computers equipped with Internet access and printers
- Computer disks
- Writing paper
- Pencils

Activity

Students will love hunting for their favorite cartoon characters on the Internet!

1 Before doing this activity you will need to show your students how to connect to the Internet and use search engines to locate information on the World Wide Web.

2 Have your students, either individually or in pairs, connect to the Internet.

3 Ask each one to use a search engine (i.e. Lycos, Yahoo, Excite) to find a picture of a favorite cartoon character. Do any necessary screening of Web sites before you do this activity.

4 Next have students save the image to a disk and print it. Then have them create comic strips or write stories using the character.

5 Finally, be sure to teach your class how to exit the Internet and correctly shut down the computers, if necessary.

It is usually easy for students to learn computer skills. These Internet searching skills will come in handy throughout the year.

FACT: Mark Hamill, Luke Skywalker in the movie Star Wars, has provided the voices for over 400 cartoons since he made the movie.

Date Used   Notes

©TREND

School Mates

Materials & Prep

- Photos of each student and school staff member
- Index cards
- Rubber cement

Activity

Students will learn to recognize their classmates and school staff members while honing their concentration skills in this matching game.

1 Prepare this game by taking individual photos of each student in your class and school staff members. Take the film to a photo lab where they offer double prints for free. Mount each photo on a separate index card.

2 This game works best if students play it in groups of two, three, or four. Choose the groupings that work best with your class.

3 There are two ways students can play with these cards.

- The first way to play is for one player to shuffle all of the cards and spread them out face down on a table or floor. Each player in the group then takes a turn choosing cards to turn over in an effort to make a match. In addition to finding two identical photos, the student must name the pictured person in order to claim the match. Students who make matches get to continue taking turns until they turn cards over that don't make a match or can't name the person in matching photos. The student with the most matches at the end wins the game.

- A little later in the year play the game in a similar manner, with a twist. Now, take one of each picture out of the deck and replace it with a card with the student's name written on it. To make a match, students must match a photo with the written name of the person depicted.

Students will enjoy playing this matching game all year long!

Date Used   Notes

Top That Number!

Materials & Prep

- An old copy of a telephone book
- A calculator for every one or two students
- Pencils

Activity

Students will practice addition, estimation, and calculator skills using phone books. Students who love a challenge will be wild about this activity.

1 Tear out several pages of an old telephone book. Give one page to each student.

2 Challenge the students with these math problems using the phone numbers on their pages.

- Try to find the phone number on each page whose seven numerals add up to the highest total. Explain that it would be very time-consuming to either add them all manually or use a calculator for each one. Instead, the fastest way is to do quick estimates. Talk about how estimating might be done with the phone numbers. If the first three digits are all the same, what fourth digit numerals will result in the highest sums? Circle the sums you think are the highest, and check those with a calculator.

- Use the same strategies to find the phone number with the lowest total when adding the seven numerals.

- Choose ten or more phone numbers from your list. Take the hyphen out and rewrite them as regular whole numbers (555-9823 would be 5,559,823). Then put the numbers in order from highest to lowest.

- Use those same phone numbers and jumble the numerals to make the highest possible number (555-1242 would be 5,554,221). Now put these in order from highest to lowest.

Students will have a great time finding high and low numbers. Challenge them to create other math problems using the phone book pages.

FACT: The first telephone book was published in New Haven, Connecticut, and had only 50 names in it.

Date Used   Notes

Go Me! Pennants

Materials & Prep

- Paper, fabric, or cardboard pennants (see illustrations)
- Markers, paints, colored pencils, and/or crayons
- Scissors
- Glue/paste
- Fabric markers or paints
- Glitter
- Fabric scraps
- Old magazines to cut apart
- Other types of media (optional)

Activity

Creating "Go Me! Pennants" is a fun way for students to introduce themselves to their new classmates, teacher, and the school. This activity will invite each student to create a pennant that will show everyone who they are and what makes them special.

1 Tell students that they will be creating a pennant that will tell people about themselves. Pose some questions that they might want to "answer" on their pennant. What is your favorite food? What sports do you play? What do you look like? What is your best subject? Who are the people in your family?

2 Lay out the paper, cardboard, or fabric pennants. Allow students to choose the materials they will use to make their pennants.

3 When students have completed this project, there are several ways to share their masterpieces.
- Give students the option to talk about their pennants in front of the class.

- Hold one pennant up at a time and have students guess the significance of items pictured.

- Hang the pennants in the room or hall for everyone to see.

As proud fans might display the pennants of teams they follow or root for, you too can display the pennants of your students who will make you proud this year.

Date Used	Notes

Spell-Binding Fun

Materials & Prep

- Pencils
- Notebook paper or computer
- Graph paper
- Copy of the class roster for each student

Activity

Kids love to see their names in print and everyone wants to have his or her name spelled correctly. To help everyone, use names for the first spelling list of the year. Throughout the week, use the following activities to help students learn the names and spellings. For an extra challenge, use last names as well.

1 Have your students try this jumble activity. On the board, sheet of paper, or on a computer screen, mix up the letters of a name to form a jumbled word. Leave a space under the jumbled word for the students to write the correct spelling. (Example: 1. tujnis [Justin], 2. zabetileh [Elizabeth].

tujnis
Justin

2 Another fun activity is a crossword puzzle. On a sheet of graph paper, connect the names of the students, going across and down the paper. Using another sheet of graph paper, draw boxes around the spaces with letters to make your crossword puzzle. Then, number the squares as you would a regular crossword puzzle, starting at the top left and numbering across and down the page. Now comes the fun part. Make up a clue for each student to correspond with the name in the puzzle.

3 One more spelling activity is Speed Word. This not-usually-quiet game involves two teams. Each team has one member go to the board. You say the name of a student on your spelling list. The first one at the board to correctly spell the name and put down the chalk or marker gets a point for his or her team.

Having students learn how to spell each others' names is an excellent ice breaker and will help everyone learn names. Students will also enjoy sharing information about themselves during the week to help others remember them!

Date Used   Notes

©TREND

Kite Poems

Materials & Prep

- Pencils
- Lined paper
- Crayons/markers
- Drawing or construction paper
- Fabric, ribbon and/or crepe paper

Activity

This art project is also a lesson in poetry and the parts of speech. In addition, it is a good way to get to know your students and for them to get to know each other.

Before students begin writing, review adjectives, action verbs, and nouns. When students have a grasp of these concepts, have them create their own poem that fits this structure:

Line 1: your name

Line 2: two adjectives that describe you

Line 3: three action verbs having to do with you

Line 4: create two adjective/noun combinations

Line 5: three more action verbs

Line 6: two new adjectives

Line 7: your last name

Students should write their rough draft on scratch paper, edit and revise as needed, and then transfer it to construction paper for their final draft. The poem is in the shape of a kite. Write the example shown on the board to help kids visualize how their kite poems might look.

Students use their creativity to make their kites unique, just like themselves, using markers, crayons, and other media. Ribbon, fabric, or crepe paper will make wonderful kite tails. Display the kites in your classroom by hanging them from the ceiling or creating a display on the walls.

These works of art will be an excellent reminder of how every student can soar in your classroom!

Sarah

happy, cheerful

helping, drawing, playing

excellent gardener, colorful artist

practicing, planting, painting

smart, talented

Levinson

Date Used   Notes

Stump the Teacher

Materials & Prep

- Index cards
- Pens/pencils
- Stopwatch
- Pretend money
- Four of five sets of textbooks and/or workbooks from your students' previous grade level

Activity

You won't believe how students enjoy reviewing the previous year's curriculum in this activity!

1 Obtain four or five copies of the curricular materials that the students used the previous school year, such as textbooks and workbooks.

2 Divide your students into the same number of small groups as the number of subject areas you wish to review. For instance, if you want to work on spelling, math, social studies, and science, you would split your class into four groups. Give each group five index cards.

3 Tell your students that they are to review the curricular materials and write five questions, one per index card, in an effort to stump the teacher. They will be eager to review materials in order to accomplish this task!

4 Ask teams to rank their questions in order of difficulty and to write $100.00 on the back of the easiest one, up to $500.00 on the most difficult question. When all teams are done, arrange cards in a column from easiest to hardest.

Math	Language	Spelling	Social Studies	Science
$100	$100	$100	$100	$100
$200	$200	$200	$200	$200
$300	$300	$300	$300	$300
$400	$400	$400	$400	$400
$500	$500	$500	$500	$500

5 Choose a student to be the host and another to be the banker, and let the games begin! As you answer questions, require the team that wrote the question to find the correct answer in the materials to check your answer. When you get an answer right, you receive the amount of money written on the back of the card. If you get an answer wrong, you must pay the amount written on the back of the card.

6 Students can add up your winnings at the end of the game.

Later in the year, create a similar game for your students to play. Challenge them to earn more than you did!

Date Used   **Notes**

Silhouette Collage

Prep

...nstruction

...r

...t least one
...dents)

- Scissors
- Glue/paste

Activity

This art activity will boost self-esteem and creativity, and make a lovely display in your room.

1 Begin with pairs of students making silhouettes of each other. The best way to do this is to tape a sheet of construction paper vertically on the wall, at the height of the student. The student whose silhouette is being created stands with one shoulder to the paper. That student's partner turns on an overhead projector facing the student, creating a shadow on the black paper. The partner traces the shadow line with a pencil while the other student stands still. Repeat these steps to create the other partner's silhouette on another piece of paper.

2 Have the students find and carefully cut out pictures or words from the magazines that describe themselves: favorite foods, places, activities, symbols, or words describing what they are like.

3 Cut out the silhouette and paste the magazine cutouts all over it. The pictures should overlap slightly, and cover much of the silhouette, except for a space at the bottom where kids should add their names.

Display these amazing works of art in your classroom or in a commons area in the school.

FACT: The silhouette on the Major League Baseball logo is Harmon Killebrew. The silhouette on the NBA logo is Jerry West.

Date Used   Notes

Your Self Crest

Materials & Prep

- One copy of the "Who Are You?" reproducible for each student
- Markers/crayons/colored pencils
- Scissors
- Glue (optional)

Activity

This activity will clarify some values for your students, and it will provide a new and artistic way to introduce themselves.

1 Begin this activity by asking your group a series of questions. What is a crest? (*Crests were used in Medieval times, like a coat of arms, as an identifying emblem on a knight's helmet.*) How does a crest symbolize what a person values or that person's history? (*A crest depicts things that are important to an individual and many times tell you about his or her family and past.*) Discuss with your students the word values. What are important values in our society? (*Discuss your rules in school and laws the students know about.*) What do each of your student's value? Will they be the same from person to person?

2 Make copies of the outline crest reproducible on the next page. Have students follow the directions to complete each quadrant of the crest.

3 After the students fill out each section and color it, have them cut it out to be displayed in your room. You could also glue the crests to covers of folders or autobiography projects.

Date Used   Notes

Who Are You?

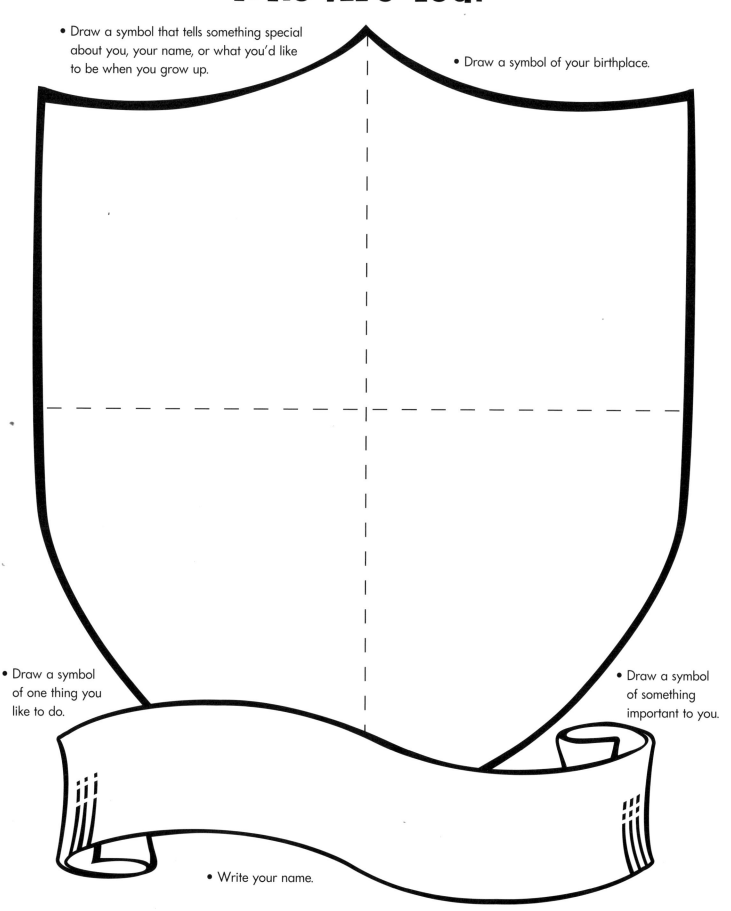

- Draw a symbol that tells something special about you, your name, or what you'd like to be when you grow up.

- Draw a symbol of your birthplace.

- Draw a symbol of one thing you like to do.

- Draw a symbol of something important to you.

- Write your name.

Shirt Tales

Materials & Prep

- Crayons/markers
- Cord or rope
- Clothespins
- One copy of the "My Favorite T-Shirt" reproducible for each student

Activity

Here is a fun and easy activity that will allow your students to really express themselves.

1 On the day you plan to begin this activity, have each student wear his or her favorite T-shirt to school. Give each student an opportunity to explain why the shirt is his or her favorite and what it means to him or her. Be sure to check your school policy on types of shirts that may be prohibited.

2 Give each student a copy of the "My Favorite T-Shirt" reproducible sheet. Have the students decorate the T-shirts with drawings that include clues about who they are. They may want to include their hobbies, interests, family, or cultural heritage.

3 To display the finished shirts, hang a cord or rope from one side of the room or hallway to the other side. Hang the T-shirts with clothespins for an unusual, charming display that celebrates the uniqueness of your students. Before hanging the shirts on the line, you may want to have a contest to see how many kids can be identified from what they represented on the T-shirts. If kids have added their names to the shirts, cover the names while guessing whose shirt it is.

My Favorite T-Shirt

Date Used   Notes

My Favorite
T-Shirt

Wanted Posters

Materials & Prep

- Construction paper
- Markers/crayons/colored pencils
- Pencils
- Camera and film (optional)

Activity

A funny way to show off your students' self portraits and learn more about them is to make wanted posters. Explain first that wanted posters are used to help law officials locate runaway criminals. These posters help to show what an individual looks like, as well as sharing some vital statistics: height, eye color, hair color, etc. Be sensitive to the fact that some statistics may be touchy to some students, such as weight. Try to avoid those on your posters. Using the wanted posters to convey positive messages makes for a fun activity!

1 Using the top 2/3 of a piece of paper, attach photographs you have taken of your students, or have the students create their own self portraits. Make sure, if students are drawing their portraits, that they add color and detail so that others will easily identify them. The word "Wanted" should appear across the top of the page.

Wanted: Mia Vang

- ➤ **Mia Vang Wanted For:** Mrs. Grant's Top Math Team.
- ➤ **Description:** 4'10", 10 years of age. Brown eyes, long black hair.
- ➤ **Last seen:** with best friend Tina Murray in choir room. Wearing lucky locket and tennis shoes.
- ➤ **Reward:** a friendship bracelet and a cheerful smile!

2 The bottom 1/3 of the paper should include information which will help others clearly identify the student.

3 Display the Wanted Posters in your classroom, the hallway, or in a common area in the school.

Students in your class and others will have fun reading the positive posters your students create.

Date Used   Notes

Who I am!

Materials & Prep

- Teacher-created inventory

- Pencils

To get started on this activity, choose questions from the list below and/or add your own to make an inventory for your students. Allow room for the students to write answers for the questions you choose.

Activity

Here is a quick get-to-know-you activity that will help you learn some very important things about your students. The more you know about each child in your classroom, the easier it will be to build rapport with her or him and talk about personal experiences.

The following is a list of many different types of questions that you might choose to ask your students. The questions range from factual information to personal preferences. When making your own inventory, choose those questions that you are interested in and put together a great get-to-know-you activity.

Sample questions:

- What is your name?
- What is your date of birth?

- List your home address and phone number(s).
- What are your parent's first and last names?
- What are your parent's numbers: work, cellular phone, pager, email?
- List your siblings names, ages, schools they go to, teacher's name(s) if they are in your school.
- Have you ever received any trophies, awards, or honors? What were they for?
- What are your hobbies?
- What is your favorite book?
- What is your favorite academic subject in school?
- Are there any subjects in school that give you trouble?
- What are you best at?
- What is your secret ambition?
- List three goals you have for yourself this year.
- What qualities do you look for in a friend?
- Why do your friends like you?
- Tell about a news event that you heard about this summer.
- What is your most-prized possession?
- Who is your personal hero?
- Do you have any hidden talents?
- What do you see yourself doing in 20 years?
- What do you expect from your teacher(s) this year?

Date Used   Notes

_____   _____

_____   _____

_____   _____

People Puzzle

Materials & Prep

- A large sheet of white tag board
- Crayons/markers
- Scissors
- Camera and film (optional)

Before you are ready to do this activity with your students, prepare the sheet of tag board to make a giant puzzle. Cut it into the shape of your choice. Then cut the large shape into smaller pieces (one for each student). Mark one side of each piece so that students know where to draw.

Activity

Every person is important to the class. The teacher and each student adds unique qualities to the whole. What makes each student important? You'll find out in this fun and "puzzling" activity.

1 Cut the number of pieces you'll need to give one piece to each student and have one for yourself.

2 Put a small mark on the side of the piece you want the children to decorate so the puzzle will fit back together.

3 There are several different things that you can have the students do with their puzzle pieces. Choose from the following or other ideas you have:

- Put student pictures on each piece.
- Decorate with icons connected with hobbies or favorite activities.
- Describe himself or herself.
- Draw family and friends.

4 Have the students introduce themselves by talking about their puzzle pieces. The information on the puzzle piece is helpful in learning about individual students.

5 Now the fun begins! Start the assembly of the puzzle. Watch the group dynamics involved in completing the puzzle. When the puzzle is done, there are several ways to use it in your classroom:

- Display the completed puzzle on a wall in your classroom.
- Laminate the pieces and use them as a center activity.
- Use the puzzle at parent events, such as an open house or parent-teacher conference.

Date Used   Notes

Cookie Contraptions

Materials & Prep

- *Frog and Toad Together* by Arnold Lobel

- Mousetrap game, ask one student to bring in a copy if he or she has the game

- Model building materials (optional)

- Drawing paper

- Pencils (optional)

Activity

After reading a well-loved story, students will design their own Rube Goldberg-style inventions.

1 Read to your class the story "Cookies" from *Frog and Toad Together*. In this story, Frog and Toad have trouble finding the willpower to stop eating cookies. They devise elaborate ways to hide the cookies from themselves. In the end, they fail.

2 Next, talk about Rube Goldberg. Explain that he is an artist who designs very complicated contraptions that perform simple tasks. If you have the game Mousetrap, set it up to show the students a Rube Goldberg-type invention in action, or search on the Internet for a site dealing with Rube Goldberg.

3 Tell students that they are to design similar contraptions to keep the cookies from Frog and Toad.

4 Depending on the amount of time you wish to spend, students can either design the contraptions on paper or create working models.

Don't be surprised to find some of your students studying more about Rube Goldberg or designing more inventions!

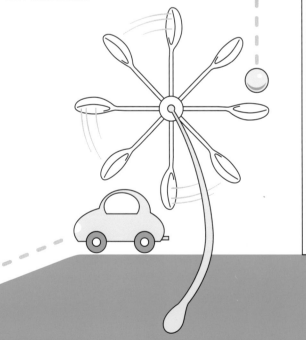

Date Used	Notes

Graduation Time Capsule

Materials & Prep

- One copy of "Time Capsule" sheet for each student
- One copy of "All About Me" sheet for each student (page 72)
- Drawing paper
- Shoe boxes
- String

Activity

This is often a favorite project with the parents. It is an excellent activity for the entire class to work on, and it will be a fun time capsule to be opened upon high school graduation.

1 At the start of the year label a shoebox for each child.

2 Send home the "Time Capsule" letter with each student. This letter will help explain the project to the parents and tell them how they can help build an exciting keepsake. Let parents know that, if they would like to add to the capsule, they are welcome to send things with their children to school or bring them in themselves.

3 What to include in the time capsule:

- Pictures of the children during the school year. Two or three pictures per student is great. Include a class picture in each capsule too.

- At least one sample of the child's art, math work, writing, and science work, as well as other academic papers.

- A copy of the "All About Me" sheet completed by the individual student.

4 At the end of the year, ask parent volunteers to wrap the boxes for safe keeping. Attach a ribbon to each with a tag that says: "To be opened on _____'s high school graduation day."

Tips:
- Many pictures will likely feature more than one student. It saves in the long run to make double prints.

- For the class photo take a roll of pictures and get double prints rather than making reprints of just one photo.

- Ask parents to donate film and help with developing costs.

By the end of the year you will have collected many different important momentos of each child's year.

Date Used   Notes

_____   _____

_____   _____

©TREND

Time Capsule

__ / __ / __

Dear Parent or Guardian,

Your child is a part of a very special class, the graduating class of _____.

To commemorate this year and the graduation event, we are planning a special project. We are making a time capsule for each child, to be opened when he or she graduates from high school. By the end of this year, the capsule will include a picture of your child in ____ grade, writing samples, and other surprises.

To accomplish our plans, we are asking for some help from you:

1. Please send a shoe box (also known as a time capsule) to school. Label the box with your child's name.

2. Please write your child a personal letter for him or her to open at high school graduation. Date it and tell him or her anything you wish. Please seal it and put your child's name on the outside of the envelope.

3. You could also include an artifact, such as a family picture, a list of things your child has done this year, or whatever you think would be fun to have inside the time capsule.

Please have your letter and box to school by _____. Thank you for your help in making this special project possible.

Sincerely,

Dear Jim,
I know that you will be

Jim Smith

All About Me

All about me in the year _____

1. I like to eat_____

2. I like to play_____

3. On T.V. I watch _____

4. My favorite movie is _____

5. My best friend is _____

6. When I grow up I want to be a _____

_____

7. On separate pieces of paper trace around your feet and your hands, one at a time.

8. Use a string to measure your height and tape it here.

Temperature Graph

Materials & Prep

- Thermometer
- Butcher paper
- Markers/crayons
- A device for finding out about the weather each day (see ideas below)

Activity

Keeping track of the temperature is a great on-going activity. It provides experience in graphing, comparing, and gathering data from many sources.

1 Before you get started determine how you will verify the temperature each day.

- Obtain a local weather phone number.

- Watch a weather channel on TV.

- Find an Internet site that gives current temperature.

- Check in a newspaper. (It will list previous day's temperatures.)

- Have a thermometer installed outside the building.

Talk to the students about weather and exchange stories about times when it was very hot or very cold. Show them a thermometer and discuss how to read it. Ask the students if they know why the weather changes like it does. (*Because of the tilt of the earth during different seasons, parts of the earth are closer to the sun than others. For example, during North America's winter it is tilted further away from the sun causing colder weather. At that same time, South America is closer to the sun and is in its warmer, summer season.*)

2 On butcher paper make a graph with every ten degrees labeled across the bottom in a different color. Label the left scale with the days of the month.

3 Pick a convenient and consistent time to check the temperature each day.

4 Color in the square on the graph above the temperature of the day.

5 Predict the color that will "win" each month. As the year goes on it's amazing to see the guesses improve.

Date Used	Notes

Cookie Count

Materials & Prep

- Chocolate chip cookies
- Your favorite chocolate chip cookie recipe and ingredients
- 2 large mixing bowls
- Measuring cups
- Measuring spoons
- 2 wooden spoons
- Oven

Activity

Use this delicious activity to practice estimation, measuring, division, and averaging skills.

1 Hold up a chocolate chip cookie for the class to see. Ask students to estimate how many chocolate chips are in that cookie and record each student's estimate on the board.

2 Give each student a chocolate chip cookie to look at closely. Allow students to revise the estimate made before, now that they have had a closer look at a similar cookie.

3 Tell the students to eat the cookies carefully, trying to count the number of chocolate chips as they go. Then let them make more

revisions of the estimates. Compare the estimates at the three stages.

4 Make a batch of chocolate chip cookies with the class. Allow students to take turns doing the measuring.

5 When it's time to add the package of chocolate chips, ask the students for ways to determine how many chips are in the bag. Record the estimated number of chips in the bag, and proceed with baking the cookies.

6 When the cookies are baked, count how many cookies there are and record that number. See if your students can figure out how many chips are in each cookie. How does this number compare to the previous estimates? The next step is for students to eat one more cookie, again counting the number of chips as they eat.

7 Show students how they can average all of the estimates they came up with to arrive at a "best guess." To find this average, add all estimates and divide by the number of estimates made. This average number of chips in a chocolate chip cookie is a "best guess."

This activity, which includes the popular activities of cooking and eating, provides excellent concrete experiences with estimation.

Date Used   Notes

Classroom Newsletter

Materials & Prep

- A computer with printer
- Photocopy machine
- Paper

Activity

You can use this activity to get students started on a project to produce a weekly classroom newsletter.

1 Prior to beginning this activity, make sure that both you and your students are familiar with the basics of your computer's word processing program. Students will need to be able to compose a document, save it to a disk, and print it.

2 Each day assign a different student to make that day's entry in the class log, a file you created on a disk. Students should record the highlights of that day, special events, and any other interesting news about the day at school. Then save the entry on a disk. Computer-savvy students may wish to add graphics. At the end of the week, you can add any school announcements or notes you want to make to parents, such as homework or field trip information.

3 Assign an editor, or editors, the last school day of the week to proofread the weekly entries, arrange the copy in the page format you are using, and print the newsletter.

4 Make photocopies of the newsletter for all your students to enjoy and take home for their parents to read.

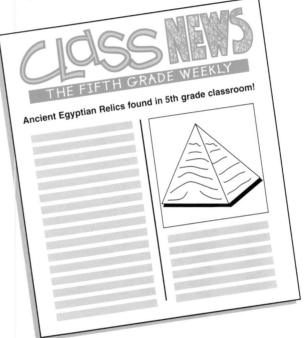

This activity keeps parents informed, reinforces computer skills, and gets your students writing and editing.

FACT: President John F. Kennedy could read four newspapers in 20 minutes.

FACT: A newspaper publisher once fired Walt Disney because he had no good ideas.

Date Used   Notes

You Can Count on Our Playground!

Materials & Prep

- Count on Our Playground! teacher-created worksheet.
- Pencils
- Calculators (optional)
- Tape measures/rulers (one for every two students)

You will need to spend some time out on your playground writing your own personal "Count on Our Playground" worksheet. The following is a list of possible questions for your worksheet. Choose the best questions for your students' abilities and add your own questions to personalize the list to fit your playground.

1. How many vertical bars are there on the playground structure?

2. What is the length of the bridge?

3. How many swings are there on the playground?

4. What is the perimeter of the sand box?

5. What is the total number of chain links used on one swing?

6. How many horizontal bars are there on the playground structure?

7. What is the total number of landings on the playground structure?

8. How many slides are there on the playground?

9. What is the length of one slide?

10. What is the height of one picnic table?

11. What is the circumference of the trash can?

12. What is the diameter of the center circle in the basketball court?

13. What is the width of the sidewalk?

14. What is the area of one window of the school?

15. What is the area of the four-square court?

16. How long is the hopscotch court?

Activity

Your students will love getting out onto the playground for a few days during math class for this fun and "telling" math activity. The playground activity is a wonderful way to begin to assess your students' math abilities. When creating your worksheet, use several different types of questions that are within, and slightly above, the regular abilities of students in the grade level you teach. This will allow you to see what your students are capable of doing and where individuals may struggle.

1 Pair your students so that two students work together on this project. Decide what the best types of pairings are, avoiding "trouble spots" and helping those students who may need a partner with a little more math sense.

Date Used   Notes

2 Explain that you will be going on the playground for this activity and then proceed to go over safety rules that they must follow.

3 Pass out one worksheet to every student. All students should have their own copy and should write each answer on their own paper. Ask that before they begin finding the actual answers, they, as a pair, make estimates for all of the answers. This will promote another skill, and it will be fun for them to see how close their guesses are.

4 Now let them loose. It is helpful, if you have a very large group, to section off the different parts of the playground and the different parts of your worksheet. This will allow some groups to work in area A while other groups are in area B. This will help students spread out and avoid hearing other's answers. Blow the whistle half way through the period and have students switch areas.

5 Depending on the number of questions on your worksheet, this activity may take a couple of class periods to complete. When students are done, after you have checked their work, pull the group together and compare estimates and answers.

This activity should give you a variety of information that you will be able to use throughout the school year. You'll learn who works well with others and who has a difficult time. You'll find out who can work in an open setting and who needs more structured surroundings. And finally, you'll learn what kinds of math skills the students in your class have and what you'll need to work on during the year.

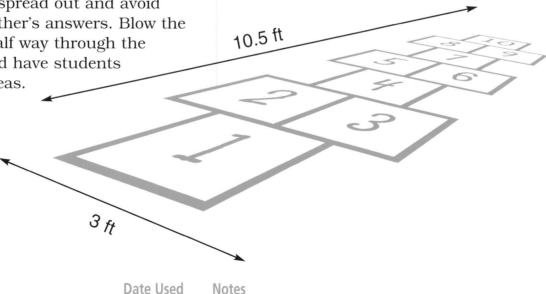

10.5 ft

3 ft

Date Used   Notes

Friendly Food

Materials & Prep

- Friendship bread recipe and ingredients
- Chart paper
- One quart-sized plastic bag for each student
- Markers
- Large plastic bowl
- Wooden spoon
- Fruit and store-bought desserts brought by students
- Copies of "Friendly Food" reproducible

Activity

Students cooperate to prepare a friendly, delicious lunch.

1 Start working on your friendship lunch ten days in advance by starting friendship bread. This recipe requires a starter. Ask around to see if someone has some, or order from Armchair World at (310) 477-8960. Copy the recipe on chart paper and explain the importance of following the directions carefully. If you would like, add a science experiment to this activity by letting students make two batches—one following the recipe exactly, and one altering it, such as using metal utensils. Then compare the results.

2 Send a letter home to parents explaining that your class will be enjoying a friendship lunch in ten days. While students need not bring lunch money or cold lunch that day, they do need to bring one piece of fruit and a gift-wrapped individual dessert.

3 On the designated day, bake the bread as directed and make a friendship fruit salad by preparing and combining the fruit students brought from home. During this preparation, display a piece of rotten fruit, explaining that it can ruin the whole bowl of fruit, just as one student can ruin an experience for the whole class. Have extra fruit and dessert on hand in case any students forget to bring items from home.

4 After enjoying the fruit salad and bread, kids can participate in a dessert exchange. Be sensitive to any food allergies students may have.

5 Send each student home with containers with equal amounts of friendship dough starter and copies of the bread recipe.

This delicious activity will be fondly remembered for a long time!

Date Used   Notes

Friendly Food

Amish Friendship Bread
Makes 2 loaves

Day 1: Put live starter in a bowl.

Days 2–5: Stir with a wooden spoon.

Day 6: Add one cup each of flour, sugar, and milk. Stir with a wooden spoon.

Days 7–9: Stir with a wooden spoon.

Day 10: Stir in one cup each of flour, sugar, and milk. Put one cup into each of three separate containers, such as margarine tubs or quart-sized plastic bags.* Give one cup of this batter and a copy of the recipe to each of three friends. To the balance of the batter, mix in one cup oil, three eggs, ½ cup milk, and one teaspoon vanilla.

In a separate bowl, mix one cup flour, one cup sugar, 1 ½ teaspoons baking powder, ½ teaspoon salt, ½ teaspoon baking soda, one cup chopped nuts, two teaspoons cinnamon, and one (about 5 oz.) box of instant vanilla pudding.

Add the dry ingredients to the wet ingredients and pour the mixture into two greased loaf pans. Bake at 325° F for one hour.

Do not use metal bowls or utensils. Use plastic or glazed ceramic bowls, and do not refrigerate.

*When making this recipe with your class, you may want to put a small amount of starter into containers for each student to take home along with the recipe.

Index